All That Matters: Memoir From the Wellness Community of Greater Boston

©2006 Peggy Rambach
The Paper Journey Press
an Imprint of Sojourner Publishing, Inc.
Wake Forest, NC USA

All rights reserved. Printed in the United States of America

No part of this book may be reproduced or transmitted in any form or by any means, electronic or mechanical, including photocopying, recording, or by any information and storage and retrieval system, without written permission from the publisher, editor, or pertinent author.

Views expressed within these pages are those of the authors and do not necessarily represent the views of Sojourner Publishing, Incorporated or its imprints.

Cover photo by Gretje Ferguson
Cover design by Mark Nedostup
Author photo by Sarah Putnam

The Paper Journey Press: www.thepaperjourney.com
First trade paperback edition
Manufactured in the United States of America

Special Thanks
The Wellness Community of Greater Boston
Echo Bridge Office Park
1039 Chestnut St.
Newton Upper Falls, MA 02464
617.332.1919
www.wellnesscommunity.org

Library of Congress Control Number: 2006932254
International Standard Book Number (ISBN) 0-9773156-7-3

All That Matters

*Memoir From the
Wellness Community of Greater Boston*

Edited by Peggy Rambach

The Paper Journey Press
Wake Forest, NC

To Peggy Rambach who helped each of us find the way through our stories, letting them lead us where they wanted to go, and for encouraging us to keep them alive.

To the Wellness Community for giving us the opportunity and environment to face our cancer together.

To the memory of Leo Sicuranza who encourages us to live each day as fully as we can.

All That Matters

Acknowledgments

We are all deeply grateful for the generosity of Françoise Hul who funded the Wellness Community Memoir Writing Workshop. The Wellness Community of Greater Boston has been in operation for twelve years and was started by Gilda Radnor's best childhood friend after Gilda's death from ovarian cancer.

I want to thank Harriet Berman, Program Director of the Wellness Community, for her enthusiasm and collaboration on this project. And I wish to thank all of the members of the Wellness Community Writing Workshop for the tremendous energy, commitment and joy they brought to every class and to the achievement of the work in this collection.

The Wellness Community is a 501(c)3 non-profit organization with a mission to provide free professional support, education and stress management services to people with cancer and their families. The first Wellness Community was started more than twenty years ago in Santa Monica, California and there are currently twenty-two Wellness Communities nation-wide and two overseas. Each Wellness Community is self-sustaining and relies on contributions from individual, corporate and foundation donors to raise money in order to provide services.

In addition, I wish to thank Wanda Wade Mukherjee, managing editor of the Paper Journey Press, for supporting our endeavor to make this book a reality.

Peggy Rambach
Andover, Massachussetts
January 2006

Introduction

At the first session of the Wellness Community's Memoir Writing Workshop, the word "cold" came up. How cold it was in the examination rooms. How cold it was outside of Radiology. "I wanted to tell everyone to wear warm-up suits," said Christine Micklitsch of her less experienced waiting-room companions. Cold tables, cold instruments against warm skin. Room thermostats set low for the optimal performance of the machines inside them and only johnnys to protect the people who would go inside the machines. The johnny: a garment that was universally reviled. "Who designed those things, anyway?" someone asked and everyone laughed.

The room was filled with a long and polished conference table, light from the two walls of windows that looked out over trees and rocks and the Charles River, and a group of people whose shared experience and purpose generated a camaraderie that guaranteed cold would never be part of this experience. Hard work—yes. Some frustration, it's true. One student did confess to groaning and temporarily abandoning (or maybe throwing) her manuscript across her living room when she saw how thoroughly I had covered it in roller-ball green.

But the participants in this writing class were not going to experience the emotional catharsis that comes from writing in free-form. No. If they were going to experience any kind of benefit, therapeutic or otherwise, it was going to come from a strict adherence to discipline. Mine was the boot camp, you might say, of support center writing workshops. But this was only because we were writing in the literary form called memoir, and because we were writing for an audience. And that is hard.

Here at the Wellness Community was a roomful of people who shared an intimate knowledge of how life is inclined to distribute loss, pain, hardship and heartache in the manner of chicken feed. You'd think, given their raw material and enthusiasm, the actual writing would be a cinch. But the more immediate and deep a story's emotional significance, the more challenged I am to show the writer how to write it well.

Writing anything feels like jumping off a boat into the middle of the ocean, so of course you want to grab onto something that promises to keep you afloat. Well, chronology always appears to be just the thing. The linear approach. After all, our lives are stories that unfold in the manner of a timeline: we're born, we live, we die. So why not begin all stories at the beginning and just record one part of it to the next, to the next, until there are no more parts to record. But unfortunately what you get is something about as interesting to read as a Palm Pilot calendar; the experience so recorded might be good for posterity, but not for meaning.

So if chronology is out, then what? Well, that's where all the green ink comes in. You chop. You add. You rearrange. And you begin at the beginning again and again and again to find a path to the single moment, the sole image that will, when rendered with honesty and specificity, open up to reveal to both writer and reader a great surprise: the moment when the personal truth becomes universal.

Christine Micklitch's hat, for instance, becomes *her*, who she was before she had cancer, and who she will never be again. The feel of breeze in a place Pat Connolly never felt it before hints of new discoveries made in unexpected ways; Patricia Griecci's inexplicable preference for the color pink becomes the first sign of her emergence into a life she never wanted, but nevertheless must live. The touch of Elaine Brilanstone's mother's hand on her hair, the feel of Harriet Berman's daughter in her arms, hands stained with blackberry juice in Sazi Marden's memoir of her childhood, Roberta Frechette's singing frogs, and the taste of a cookie that Cheryl Sisel eats with her grandchildren—every image speaks of more. A wedding charades as a funeral in Debbie Hemley's memoir, "Veteran." And in the opening of a piece that Leo Sicuranza wrote in the only class he could attend, a hospital sign that says "Patients" shows how we should never be defined.

And though these writers might have thought that the drama and gravity, the beauty and personal significance of their experiences were reasons enough to make them worth writing down, they were to discover the real one by doing the hard work of the writing itself, by embarking on what writing really is: a search.

I was privileged to be the leader of their expedition.

Peggy Rambach
Andover, Massachusetts
February 2006

Table of Contents

Sylvia's House
by Deborah Hemley 1

Too Late
Pat Connolly 5

The Far West
by Sazi Marden 9

The Telling
by Harriet Berman 15

A Mother's Prayer
by Elaine Brilanstone 21

Pink
by Patricia Griecci 29

My Hat
by Christine Micklitsch 33

Frog Chant
by Roberta Frechette 43

Veteran
by Deborah Hemley 47

Simpler Now
by Pat Connolly 55

All That Matters
by Cheryl Sisel 57

Contributors 61

About the Editor 65

All That Matters

*Memoir From the
Wellness Community of Greater Boston*

Edited by Peggy Rambach

The Paper Journey Press
Wake Forest, NC

— Deborah Hemley —
Sylvia's House

When I was fifteen, two young women who lived on our block were both sick with some form of cancer. I got the message not from what was said, but what was not said, hints, and references to the "c" word. Even so, it became obvious to me that they were not going to live much longer. Darkness and sickness loomed over their families and homes, and I was afraid of them both. I didn't want to know any of the specifics or truths about their circumstances.

My mother asked me, encouraged without giving me a choice, or more accurately forced me, to visit the one woman who lived directly across the street. She said it was important to Sylvia that I did, and that seeing me would make her happy. My mother said that Sylvia often asked about me, if I was still working at the ice cream store and what I was planning to do this summer. "Besides," she said, "it's the right thing to do."

After several conversations about when I was actually going to pay this visit, I grudgingly walked across the street. The door was slightly ajar so Sylvia wouldn't have to get up to answer it. But I knocked before entering, as my mother had instructed and said, "Hi Sylvia, it's me, Debbie." "I'm in the bedroom," she said. The shades and curtains were drawn, though it was day, and the house smelled stale: mothball odor from the front closet, mildewed wall-to-wall carpeting, windows shut, not the slightest bit of fresh air, all of which to me were the signs and smells of death.

She was wearing a blue nightgown, head propped up on several sagging pillows. Her hair was uncombed and messy. It was black and speckled with gray. The dark circles under her eyes and pale, parched lips made her look older then she was. The room was quiet. No sounds of TV or radio. When I was home, sick, I always watched TV, so the silence disconcerted me. Sylvia asked me some innocuous questions about school, my plans for the summer, and I answered with whatever came into my head, all the while distracted by the thought of cancer and that she was dying from it. So I wouldn't have to look at her, I gazed instead at a painting on the wall of a woman crawling up a haystack colored hill. I didn't know what to say, what kinds of questions to ask. What could possibly be new for her? She hadn't been outside in weeks, shut off from the world, so I couldn't even marvel with her at the spring-like weather. I was afraid it might make her sad.

Up until this point, my grandfather was the only person I'd known who had died. He had a massive heart attack while playing cards in Miami Beach, Florida; so death, to me, was sudden and pain-free, and happened in a sunny warm climate.

A few weeks later Sylvia died, and afterward the feeling in the neighborhood was noticeably different. There was a hush. Kids didn't play in the middle of the street or shout to their friends. The noise came from the airplanes that flew low over our houses every day of the week, every week of the year. The body of a plane would suddenly emerge, and the sound of the engines was deafening as they descended to the runways of JFK International Airport.

The morning of the funeral, while I sat on the front steps of our house, a Boeing 727 swooped down so low that I could make out the dark blue hockey stick design on the belly, and the words Eastern Airlines. The large teardrop-shaped wings lifted their flaps and the plane roared. Sylvia's family approached the limousine dressed in fancy black clothes, clutching clusters of pink tissues.

My mother told me that in her final days, Sylvia scribbled notes to her husband and put them in closets, cabinets and drawers, places he would go after she died and be sure to find them. I heard one was in the cereal cabinet. I thought what could she have written that she couldn't have possibly said in person? Was it about Rice Krispies cereal, a list of what to buy at the supermarket? But really, I knew. She wrote "I love you, and I'll miss you, and take good care of yourself and Linda, and please, for me, move on with your life."

A few years later, I was maybe a hero. I was daydreaming out our front window when I saw smoke coming from Sylvia's house. It started as a white cloud and then rapidly darkened and billowed. And when Sylvia's husband returned home hours later, my father and a few other neighbors told him the story about the smoke, the flames, fire trucks and me, that I was the person who called the fire department. Later he came over. He looked tired and worn as we welcomed him in; we told him how sorry we were and asked him what we could do to help. After a few minutes he turned to me and said, "So you're the one who saw the fire first," but to my surprise, he didn't thank me. His face was blank except for his eyes. They were angry and sad. We heard later that the investigators determined the fire to be suspicious, so my family's theory was that Sylvia's husband had set it himself—out of grief or to collect insurance money so he could move on.

— Pat Connolly —
Too Late

The tech—tall, broad and sure-footed, strides ahead of me into the room. I scurry to keep up. Without a backward glance, she points to where I should lie, there beside the ultrasound machine. One small contraption in one quarter of a gaping room, too big to feel safe. Dormant monitors line one wall, each on its own metal cart, each sitting in a tangle of thick cords and plugs and socket panels. Shelves full of gadgets and hardware—blood pressure cuffs, silver-lidded cylinders, a couple of EKG units sprouting leads and paper tape. Too little light in here. The place is cavernous, clinical, stark.

I hesitate, wrapping my arms around my gooseflesh and the flimsy johnny. I watch the tech glide around in the chill dimness. She refills a box of purple latex gloves, flips a toggle, types in a quick message at the keyboard, all done with an assurance and cool disinterest born of repetition. She is the alpha female in her domain, working her territory. She scopes the landscapes of women's breasts, mines the monitor for clues, subdues her prey.

I feel something like panic rise in my chest. I want to break her and I want to win her, both at once, maybe get her to laugh, unmask the human lines around her mouth and eyes. I might warm her up, get her to admit the truth. "Shhhhh," she would confide, "I'm not supposed to tell, but since you're so nice…it's nothing. Don't be worried." I want to best her, to befriend her, to make her go away, to take her down at the knees. Be a rebel and simply walk out.

She ticks through her duties and says flatly, "Lie down with your left breast exposed." I slide onto the gurney. It's a block of ice under a thin sheet. I shiver. How many times has she said that? How many women have entered this place, terrified, hopeful, and gone down weeping?

"Put your left hand over your head."

I drop the left side of the johnny and obey.

She tells me to position my back against a hard foam triangle the length of my torso. My body rests unnaturally on the edge of my hip bone, not like settling down to sleep. No settling down here. I am twisted, facing the dark ceiling.

She stands above me, filling my vision. "I'll apply some gel." She squirts a stream onto my breast.

I see an opening. "This gel isn't as cold as the gel for those prenatal ultrasounds we had back then," I say, thinking: We. People like you and me. You and me, in fact. You're about my age. Remember?

When will she soften? Why won't she crack? "Oh, yeah?" is all she musters. No comfort, no trace of camaraderie. I am alone here, cold, and compromised into a half-naked pretzel pose. She shows no mercy.

She presses the transducer with her right hand onto my left breast and scopes it, moving slowly, repetitively. Her left clicks the keyboard. She's ambidextrous. Impressive.

Minutes tick by, then more and more. I hold my breath, not meaning to, then remember to breathe, forget, and hold my breath again. I feel my hip dig into steel, the tingle in my contorted arm, a lump of terror in my gut. Her pressure increases, uncomfortable, more specific. She makes a circle, a smaller one, then smaller. She finds a spot, nails it. She adds more gel, says nothing. Again. Again. Again. She types feverishly about what she sees, moves the transducer a bit. Types again. Her breath comes more rapidly. She types a final note and clicks to make the image freeze.

"You can go back to the waiting room now." She flips on lights—stinging and bright. The machinery and the paraphernalia in the room blanch. I flinch, scramble to my feet and just before I leave, I glance at the monitor. There they are, the usual streaks, dots, and striations. But there's something in the center, stunningly more distinct than all the rest. Black, dense, a jagged-edged ellipse with tentacles splayed, invading. It is no shadow. It is the enemy.

She knew all along. It's too late to make her like me, spare me, save me. In a minute, someone new will lie here. Someone else will shudder and contort and pray for mercy. But it's too late for me. It always was.

— Sazi Marden —

The Far West

On the way to Aunt Kay and Uncle Jim's I looked out of the car while Daddy drove along the Charles River. Sometimes it was calm and peaceful. Sometimes it was crowded with crew teams from Harvard, MIT and BU, all competing for space. During the winter when it was frozen, my mother and father would tell us how dangerous it was. "It may look safe," they would say, "but it won't hold you," scaring us enough to make sure that my sisters, Anne, Judy and Kay, and my brothers, Tommy, Paul, Robert and Ricky, and I would never be victims of the not-frozen-solid Charles.

To go to Natick, we drove through Watertown. In Watertown Square we'd see the waterfalls. They were our Niagara Falls, always there waiting for us. We drove by them every time we went to Natick, so they were like old friends. Next we'd go through Newton. And if it was between Halloween and the Fourth of July, we passed the BIG SANTA. He was two stories high. He permanently waved and smiled for us and we would crane our necks for as long as we could, to see him.

We drove through West Newton Square and over Commonwealth Avenue, the big fire station on our left. Then by Newton Wellesley Hospital and into Wellesley where we passed over the Charles, but the cement sides of the bridge prevented us from seeing our river. Right after Wellesley College we saw the sign, "Welcome to Natick."

About a mile down the road my father took a left at Main Street and passed the Stop and Shop where my uncle managed the meat department. Then we were in the country. There were trees everywhere, except on the big front lawns, and then we saw the big red school on the right. We knew that when we passed our mountain, which was really a large rock on the left side of the road, we'd see the house with Mary Rose and Kathleen watching out the windows for us, their Cambridge cousins. And then my father would take a left into the dirt yard, and would have barely put the car in park, when Mary Rose and Kathleen would be opening the doors. My Aunt Kay was always in the kitchen cooking brownies or Toll House cookies for us, and my Uncle Jim would be working in the garden, the hen house, or the barn. Tomatoes, corn, and green beans were the specialties of Uncle Jim's garden. In winter when my mother served us green beans she always said they were from Uncle Jim's garden, guaranteeing that we'd eat them.

My Natick relatives lived in a one family house owned by Mrs. Riley, who was not a relative. Mrs. Riley was a short, old, friendly lady who lived on the second floor. Her body leaned forward and she used a mahogany cane to hold herself up. She never left the second floor, where she had a tiny kitchen with a stove, slightly larger than my cousins' Easy Bake oven. Beside it was a small icebox on high legs. On the opposite wall there was a small Formica table and one chair. There was only enough room to pull the chair out halfway. I don't remember a sink but I do remember the sweet, spicy smell of her stuffed green peppers. Her living room, which she also used as her bedroom, was spacious. We would sit with her in her overstuffed armchairs and listen to "Queen for a Day" on the radio, sucking on confectionery coated hard candy from her fancy clear cut glass candy dish.

Also, on the second floor was my cousins' one bedroom and the one bathroom everyone shared. Traveling to the bathroom in the daytime was easy, but after dark it became an adventure and I was afraid to go upstairs alone. So usually, one of my cousins would walk up with me and talk to me through the bathroom door while she waited patiently outside.

When we first arrived, we'd all climb out of the car and run in to see what Aunt Kay was cooking for us. Then we'd run for the chicken coop, tiptoeing in so as not to disturb the hens, slowly reach under the nests to get the warm eggs, and carry our precious treasures in to Aunt Kay. Then, next, we ran down to the brook, picked spearmint leaves, rinsed them in the clear, cold, running water and chewed them. Aunt Kay said they would taste like spearmint gum but they never did. We'd just spit out bitter leaves every time. But that never stopped us from trying again on our next visit.

Sometimes Mary Rose, Kathleen, Anne, Judy and I would pack peanut butter and crackers and juice and go hiking to our mountain pretending we were in the real mountains somewhere even farther out west than Natick.

Blackberry season meant we would eat food from a tree. My aunt gave us old coffee cans and we'd run up to the bushes and start picking, get scratched on the thorns, and be horrified by the bugs we'd find crawling on the berries. We'd laugh, eat and rub our wounds all at the same time. We didn't know if the stains on our arms and hands were from blood or blackberry juice. We ate most of berries while picking but did manage to bring home a small token to be washed.

Aunt Kay and Uncle Jim always invited either Anne, Judy, or me to spend a whole school vacation week at their house. We'd sleep, sandwiched between Mary Rose and Kathleen who shared a double bed, the Natick cousins on the outside and the Cambridge cousin in the middle. We talked and giggled until Uncle Jim would holler, "Quiet down, up there. Don't make me come up," which would immediately silence us. But I always wondered what would happen if he did come up, since I had never once seen my Uncle Jim angry. Once I knew that we really had to go to sleep I would try hard to be the first because I didn't want to listen to Kathleen snore. And she, being considerate, would try to stay awake.

Aunt Kay and Uncle Jim always and forever hosted the family cook-outs. Everyone came and no one ever missed one: the eight Malden O'Brien's, the five Belmont O'Brien's, the five Flaherty's from Burlington, the seven Terrio's from Somerville, the five Le Blanc's from Cambridge and the ten Rossi's from Cambridge all made the trip to the country. Uncle Jim and Aunt Kay supplied the hot dogs, the hamburgs and the fire. Everyone else brought their specialty: Aunt Marian's potato salad, made only with Hellman's, Mummy's homemade brown beans,

Aunty Eileen's Irish bread, Aunt Therese's carrot slaw, Aunt Joan's Italian sausage and peppers and Grandma's apple pie. Normally, we didn't get to have chips and tonic, but at these shindigs, it was anything goes.

The hunt for the perfect marshmallow stick was as much fun as the toasting. It would have to be just the right length and width. We'd get to use a real knife to cut a sharp clean point. Everyone cooked their own marshmallow to suit their individual tastes; from barely brown to my favorite, burned black and bubbly.

Uncle Phil, my godfather, wrapped in a sheet and sitting in a tree, ended the cook-out by telling scary stories. All the kids, with bellies full, would get comfortable around the fire and look up into the tree. Uncle Phil's deep voice rolled over us and lulled us, but we could never really let our guard down completely because we'd know that the story was going to have a surprise ending that would make us scream. We never did figure out just when it was coming because every year the ending made us scream in a frightfully pleasant way.

How did my Aunt Kay and Uncle Jim manage to do all that work and make it seem so easy, so natural? We all miss those cook-outs. But Aunt Kay died and Uncle Jim moved to an efficiency apartment in Natick. Now there is no room for the eighty or so relatives who would love to gather around the hearth again.

— Harriet Berman —
The Telling

The room felt small. It was as if the chairs had moved in towards one another in anticipation of a job they knew was important. The windows refused to let the outside in. The silence was loud and insistent. The lights, the carpet, the fireplace, the table, all serious, focused, waiting for their instructions. But there were none, no pre-written dialogue.

Stan and I hadn't really thought about how we would do this. So we sat next to one another on the blue couch. I could feel the pillows give underneath me. I sank in. His presence next to me was the only steady thing in the room, and in this moment even that was not so steady. This was the part that from the first moment loomed largest and most terrifying for us both. For all our expertise in such matters, we were up against something that required a new roadmap and vocabulary.

Eliza sat in the tall rocking chair, nervously shifting back and forth to get comfortable. Her lanky body never looked right sitting still—the long legs and arms, the strong shoulders were more at home on the soccer field, throwing a basketball, somehow in motion. She had walked at nine months—the third child who was supposed to be mellow, and wait for everyone to do for her, had somehow turned out to be the one who couldn't wait to get moving. So here she sat, uncharacteristically still. Limbs too awkward to curl in on themselves the way I felt she would have liked at that moment.

Jonah sat next to her. He seemed comfortable, casually splayed in the other rocking chair, legs out in front of him, his oversized jeans revealing just a hint of his plaid boxer shorts below the blue hooded sweatshirt. Always the easy-going one, the confident one. Though he had grown from a teenager into a handsome, jaunty young man, newly accepted into college and music conservatory, as he sat there I saw the warm and engaging baby and toddler—the one who molded so perfectly to my arms, the boy who hated to get into trouble and had managed to avoid it well into his teenage years—either through making good choices or clever cover-ups. He waited, confident that we would take care of him and speak the plain truth of the matter and then he could be on his way.

In front of me, on the round marble table top sat a basket of stones. We had collected them over the years from various vacation spots or day trips, each marked carefully on the bottom: "Ingham Pond, '97," "Dolphin Marina, '96," "Acadia, '92," "Lucy Vincent Beach, '85." I picked up one or two and turned them over in my hands. The long silent baby grand piano sat to my right. Rarely played, it served now more as a spacious surface for family pictures. Pictures of my father, my mother, grandparents, black and white and grey alongside color photos of the children. The serious gazes of the old next to the more joyful expressions of the young.

"Mom and I were at the doctor today. She has had some tests and she needs to have surgery."

"What is it? Is it cancer?"

There it was. Eliza spoke it. No hesitation. Fear in her eyes, but clearly a need to know the whole story and know it right away.

"Yes it is," I answered. "Breast cancer."

Jonah sat silent, waiting for the information to unfold, a bit stunned, shifting his body upright in the chair.

"I'll have surgery next week, and then I'll have a few weeks before I have to do some kind of treatment. We won't know until after the surgery what that will be."

"Are you going to die?"

Again, Eliza. Cut to the chase. Tell me the most important thing right now.

"Not from this. Not anytime soon. There are good treatments and we think we found this early." It wasn't a lie. It was as much as I knew at that moment in time.

"We won't be able to host the French exchange student. But you know, Jonah, when we called Mrs. Follett, she told me she had breast cancer seven years ago—and look at her—she is fine. She is happy to talk to you whenever you want. And we know a lot of other people who have had this and are fine."

We proceeded to name names, to carefully choose people who we knew looked healthy and were likely to be fine.

"Do you have any questions?" Stan tried to look calm. The tears he had shed over the past two weeks as we waited for tests were nowhere to be seen. He was trying to be the

The Telling

steady, available dad that I so relied on.

Jonah had no questions. He feigned comfort with our explanation of things. He sat thoughtfully, privately processing it all. As outgoing as he was, easy with conversation, when confrontation of any sort entered into the mix, he turned inward. It would be some time I knew before he would be able to say what was on his mind.

Eliza spoke again. "Do we have to go tonight?"

We were expected at a Passover seder at the home of a friend of hers.

"We don't have to, but it would probably be good to be with people," I said, not really knowing if that were true. It was I who wanted a distraction. "I told them about this—so you don't need to worry. It'll be good for you to be with Dana." She looked doubtful.

"Does Jessie know?" asked Jonah.

Jessica was three thousand miles away and one month from graduation. We had not told her. We could not figure out when we would do that.

"Not yet," Stan said. "We will call her soon."

We would regret the three days it took us to work up the courage.

There was silence. A faint sound of sniffles became a soft but insistent sound of tears and Eliza's body heaved with her efforts to control them. I motioned her to come sit on the couch. Stan got up to make room for her. Jonah quietly left the room. It was a year before I knew what he felt, when he said to me, "you told us you would be fine, and I believed you."

As I lay there with Eliza, the sharp angles of her body disappeared under my hands. The tighter I held her, the harder she cried, and yet as I comforted her, she comforted me, just the feel of her in my arms and her need to be with me and to cry for what we both feared.

— Elaine Brilanstone —
A Mother's Prayer

"Where are we going?"

I was aware of the fixed, eager-to-please smile she'd affected most of her life, yet not sure if it was still a continuation of her accommodation to the world or a manifestation of what one of the doctors I'd dragged her to had called the "limitations" now of her 90-year-old brain.

"To the day care."

Silence. Not uncomfortable yet. A temporary agreement between us.

"Where are we going?"

"Oh, the place I hope you'll have fun today," I tried pushing on.

"Mmmh!" Her assessment was undeniable.

More silence. I turned toward her, but her brief critique had vanished—replaced by the ever-familiar, cooperative smile.

"Where are we going?"

I knew the question would come again and tried another tactic.

"You told me about it yesterday, and about one of the games you played. You all walked in a circle." Before I turned toward her this time, I made certain the road ahead and behind was free of oncoming or passing cars. "You remember the circle," a statement from me, not a question.

"The circle?" she repeated. This time her expression paled and her mouth hinted at a scowl.

I waited.

"If she does it again, I'm calling the cops."

"Mmm." I was noncommittal.

"The nerve."

"Uncomfortable, huh?"

"I'm calling the cops. You know what she did."

"She's your friend isn't she?"

"Friend, with a friend like that, who needs friends?"

"Oh, I think I remember."

"You bet your life. I remember that one, I remember that one."

"Mmm," I repeated as gently as possible.

"Poke a person in the back!"

"Oh, I know."

"I've a good mind…."

"Oh, we're almost there. Got to find an easy parking space so you can get out with no trouble."

Another weighty silence. I see no smile as I turn to her, instead the fixed stare of a child about to look at her surroundings.

"Oh, there's Mary, waiting for you at the door."

"Mmm, the door," she snarls.

Suspended silence, again, has the upper hand.

"Maybe if you feel like it, when I come to pick you up, we can stop for ice cream or something."

In an instant she turns toward me. "You coming in?"

"I always do. I love to see where you are during the day."

Suddenly, in an instant, that brief half-wanted image cuts me back in time to the endlessly gray, lonely schoolyard of the Quincy E. Dickerman elementary school in Roxbury. I must approach it. There's nothing else to do. It's an order. All children go to Kindergarten. As quickly as it appeared I blot the memory out and turn my full attention to my mother.

I've found a suitable parking space and I leave the car first, to open her side to carefully help her out. She is quite ambulatory but I feel the need to assist her whenever she gets out of the car. We walk the slight, concrete incline toward Mary, the day care director who stands at the open door.

"Good morning Mollie."

My mother's smile appears light-hearted, ready and eager, yet fixed to please. Mary, too, has the fixed smile, but hers I know is the inimitable professional one. How different, I wonder, are the two smiles, as I walk through the open door to a large, wide, cavernous room. Chairs in a circle, a couple of couches on one side of the wall, an old upright piano in one corner—which I hope will be a saving grace for my mother, who, as it's said, has played by ear all her life.

The piano, standing in the corner, old, wooden, battered, solitary, waiting, it seems, waiting to be brought to life. The piano is another of the current fantasies I indulge about my mother. But what is not a fantasy is her mastery of the instrument.

She and her two older sisters all learned to play with no formal teaching lessons. The oldest, Gertrude, serious and intent, went on to accompany the brash hot mama singer Sophie Tucker. Sophie may or may not have considered herself "hot," but her devil-may-care persona wowed 'em in the 20s and 30s. The next eldest sister, Aunt Rose, my favorite aunt whom I secretly and of course guiltily called my other mother, pounded her strong, hard, work-earned fingers across the keys in explosive, joyous syncopations—oh, she who makes a joyful noise—and she sure did! Then there was my mother.

Aah—my mother! The quality of her music, the drama of her playing was quite different from her older sisters. Her playing was reverentially tentative, almost hypnotic as she elongated her body sideways on the bench while at the same time arching her shoulders forward the better to meld, blend, lose herself in the melody. Her face curved in the dreamy, self-absorbed way of someone who is in her own private, safe world, who knows there is something with which she is in complete, blissful and spiritual harmony. No one, it seemed, need or should disturb that world. Those were the only times I saw my mother tranquil. And I would watch her almost surreptitiously, fearful, as if I were stealing something, or seeing something I had no right to be witness to, hoping she would, and yet sensing she would never speak about that part of her—and she never did. As if speaking about it would make it no longer be hers.

In my first conversation with Mary about my mother, I made a point of describing my mother's gift. Mary was professionally neutral. "It's good to know these things," she said as she bent over papers on her desk. "I'll talk to

Louise, in charge of programs for our clients here and see if something can be worked out so your mother can give it a whirl one of these days." I continued, "Would it be possible to work it in so she felt she had to play one song each day? Something she felt was expected of her?"

Mary was not unkind, just doing her job. "Well, we do have quite a few clients here, as you can see, and keeping all of them happy is our priority. We're aware of how most of them need encouragement. It's the name of the game."

I nodded, thanked her for listening and added, "Oh, one more thing. The poking. My mother mentioned it on the way over here this morning."

"Poking? Poking?" Mary, at first perplexed, nodded. "Oh, that. We have that kind of thing all the time, as you can imagine. Nothing to be upset about. We have them walk in a circle during the day while Louise plays a marching song. Seems Betty, whom she's made friends with, walks in back of her. You know, a playful kind of poke, the sort of thing some of them do."

I wasn't convinced, but after all, it was I who arranged to have her spend a few hours of her day here. For both our sakes. So that I would have a few hours of respite and she something with which to be occupied. I knew she would have been quite content to just sit all day in her favorite chair in my apartment.

Before I brought her to my small apartment, she'd lived alone for a few years in housing for the elderly after my father had gone willingly to the Hebrew Home of the Aged. I visited her frequently, until the day she sat quietly crying at her kitchen table—I'd never see her cry—and staring at a corner of her living room wall. She pointed to it, tearfully moaning, "There, do you see him?

"Do you see him anywhere else?" I softly asked.

"Oh yes, there, there," she turned eagerly, pointing toward the bedroom.

I knew she was talking about my father to whom she'd been married for over sixty-five years. When I saw burned pots on her kitchen stove, I knew I couldn't leave her alone anymore.

Calmly, I asked, "Why don't we go out somewhere? Or to my apartment for some supper tonight?"

Quickly, she shook her head, no. After a long silence she asked, "Will you take me right back here?"

"Of course," I lied.

During her early days with me, she worried. "Why is it so different here?" To ease her discomfort, I gave some of my furniture away and moved in some other pieces that were familiar to her, along with her small Spinet piano.

When she played a favorite of mine, "A Mother's Prayer," I knew, no matter what difficulties would inevitably arise, I'd done the right thing for her and for me. Things I never experienced before gave me a new, different mother. Her eyes would light up when I entered a room, especially when I came home after occasionally hiring a sitter, so I could attend a concert or a play.

"She hasn't slept a wink," the sitter would scold.

I'd sit on the pull-out couch she slept on and, her eyes shining in anticipation, she'd hang onto my every word as

I described the evening's events. And she'd stroke my hair when I'd lay my head in her lap.

To people who asked why I cared for her as I did, when she was never really a good mother, whatever that is, I'd explain how her mother had died when she was ten and after living from pillar to post with a succession of aunts, they married her off to the first man who answered their newspaper ad for a husband. Eventually, though, I simply said, "Why not? She's my mother."

— Patricia Griecci —
Pink

"Allison, are you ready to accept your body and move forward to having a relationship with the opposite sex?" An attractive black woman is speaking on the television. Her hair is tied up in a knot on the top of her head with tight small curls cascading down one side of her face. She looks polished, striking and strong in her red blouse with large dangling earrings and chunky necklace. Underneath is the show's title. "Starting Over," I read, "Iyanla Vanzant, Life Coach."

There is silence from the television while the camera pans over to Allison, a short-haired, timid looking blonde woman dressed casually in a green, short sleeved t-shirt. Allison takes a minute to think about her response, then quietly says that she's ready to consider moving in that direction.

But I say, "No!"

When I last looked at my scars, almost twelve months ago, the longest one looked like someone had taken a red bullet point magic marker and drawn a line right from my breast bone to my belly button. I would have fallen into the inny category before my surgery—but now my bellybutton's flat. Now, I lift my shirt and look again. The line of bright red has faded to pink and in some places I can even see the lighter shade of my own olive skin. The smaller oval egg-shaped scar on my left side has also faded, along with the surrounding scars, that were holes from drainage and feeding tubes. I still wouldn't wear a two piece bathing suit or midriff top, but the marks on my body frighten me a little less.

I used to leap out of bed at 5 a.m. and start my day walking my dogs at Veazie Street Park. I loved watching the three of them run free in the large open green field of grass, chasing squirrels, chasing each other, or just chasing their own tails. And there were my other dog walking friends too, to talk to, all of us showing up like the mailman, in every kind of weather, Bob with Buckley, a white and grey sheep dog and John with Cosmo, a brown retriever. And then me, with Spike, Sydney and Samantha.

I miss the park at different times of the day, in different seasons, how the light streamed through the early fall morning mist so peaceful and a little mysterious.

I still wake up early, but now I throw my overcoat over my pajamas and force myself just to walk the dogs around the block. On Sunday mornings, since no one is awake at 5 a.m. I give myself a break, open the front door and let them all run through the neighborhood.

Before my surgery, my morning dog walk was the way I warmed up before heading off to the Capital Club to run and swim. Then, I'd head home again, give all of us breakfast, then drive to work. I loved my work. After all, my dog Spike was my company's inspiration. The name Smiling Dog came from Spike's under bite when he smiled and how I treated him like a kid with a tail. I baked him healthy all-natural treats, created personalized feeding bowls, beds and clothing—even snow boots. And all of that turned into my vision for a Smiling Dog brand of fun dog products for crazy dog parents like me.

In the office, my day was a whirlwind of meetings with designers, stylists, writers, product developers, bakers, printers, retail buyers and investors. Out of the office I traveled to meet with retailers and show the products. And with buyers, I usually made the sale. In July 2004 I reached the pinnacle of my career at the New York Fancy Food Show. Every retail channel approached me to work with them, from food distributors to mass retailers and club stores. But then, ninety days later, my life as I knew it stopped.

I didn't know this at first, though. I was surprised when my doctor informed me that when the treatment was over, my goals should all be new, should not include resuming my old life. She said it was like I had only five coins in my pocket, so I would have to spend them wisely. One coin should be spent on eating well, another on exercise and a third on getting eight hours of sleep. I have three dogs, so I'm already broke.

Now, I spend a lot of time at home surrounded by them. My apartment is my cocoon and my dogs my comfort. And for some reason I crave pink. Before, my wardrobe was black, black and more black. But I recently bought a pink sweater. Okay, several pink sweaters, along with pink underwear, socks, and shoes. I even considered buying a pink velour sweat suit.

I never thought I'd like the color pink.

— Christine Micklitsch —
My Hat

It was another day in Naples, Florida. The girls and their father were catching shrimp off the docks behind our condo, so it was a perfect time for me to slip away for a walk to Venetian Village to window shop. There wasn't anything particular to look for other than an opportunity for some quiet time. The sun glinted off Venetian Bay, a warm breeze surrounding me, filled with the smell of bougainvillea.

I needed this break. I had started my new job at the clinic. I hardly had time to breathe in the pace of the corporate environment as it transformed into an integrated healthcare system with me as the "engineer" of physician performance and facilitator of management development. I don't think my feet had touched the ground—until this moment. Even so, I was still recovering from leaving a job I loved at the medical center. But the job had been eliminated, and I had to face that fact. Thank God I had negotiated a vacation!

I stepped off the sidewalk and onto the concrete wharf. Boats named "Hidden Treasure," "Bermuda Triangle" and "Payback" bobbed on the waves. I saw a couple boarding one of the larger ones and I wondered where other owners might be. Just ahead, I saw the busy roadway that divides Venetian Village and realized it was time to turn into the first section. I crossed the black-topped parking lot feeling the heat rise up through my sneakers.

The pastel shops were brimming with clothing and artwork I could imagine hung in grand foyers of elegant homes. I entered the under-road tunnel. This would be a skateboarder's paradise if they only allowed it. My girls loved yelling inside it to hear their voices echo. The smells of tarragon, rosemary and garlic came from the gourmet restaurants that faced the bay. I could look inside and see the delicacies on the plates and the elegant diners. I passed the fun spots that my girls enjoyed, like the metal sculpture that allowed little people to tuck inside to eat a Ben & Jerry's Chunky Monkey in the shade.

Weaving in and out of the walkways, I began to feel the heat. Even my sunglasses weren't dark enough, so I slipped into a boutique to cool down. Immediately, I smelled the customers' fine perfumes and heard clutches of women talking as they rattled the hangers against the racks. I could feel the hair on my arms rise along with goose bumps from the air conditioning. I placed my sunglasses on my head and my eyes adjusted while I walked slowly forward. The store was crowded with merchandise: cruise wear with matching accessories in tangerine, aquamarine, lime. To my left I could hear a clerk say, "How may I help you?"

"Just browsing," I responded, looking up and away to my right—and that's when I saw it, high up on a shelf, among brightly colored ones that matched the clothing below. Its subtler shades of beige and cream actually made it stand out, cool and sophisticated.

Before the clerk could drift away, I had her climbing up to reach it. Then I was holding it, feeling its firmly woven, silky texture in my hands. The threads were the colors of cappuccino froth and the darker brew beneath. They were twirled, intertwined to form concentric circles from the crown, like a snail shell. Geometric shapes decorated the main body of the hat. The brim extended about three inches from the base, much less flamboyant and unlike the others. I had seen plenty of brightly colored hats like these seeking a second life at used clothing stores, but not one like this. I recalled hats of its stature in Hollywood films over the years. This hat was like those. It felt and looked timeless.

I looked in the mirror. I was still a little sweaty. My hair needed to be combed, particularly when I compared it to the impeccably coiffed clerk. In fact, I looked a bit unkempt wearing my jogging shorts, t-shirt and sneakers, noticeably not like the other customers. Then, I placed the hat on my head and suddenly I was seductive, alluring, alive—not like a vamp, but definitely like a strong competitor—alive like I had not felt in years. I took it off my head and looked at the label, "Made in Panama"—how romantic, how Hemingwayish. Was I prepared for the price? I gathered my nerve and looked at the ticket. Under $50! I couldn't believe it. The hat was mine!

I decided to take the beach walk back. The ocean breeze was steady and I smelled the hint of fish odor in the air. I could see pelicans and sea gulls diving for their daily catch. The ocean looked like it was covered with millions of tiny floating mirrors that reflected the sun—and my hat stayed firmly on my head.

Over the years it was a constant companion; it went with me on business trips and family trips. Because it was hard to travel by air with more than one hat, I would wear two hats, putting one hat on top of the other and travel that way. This always provoked laughter from my family or business travel companions. I didn't care. I liked to wear hats and particularly that hat.

It was always the right look for every occasion and it made me feel terrific. It's not that I didn't have other hats. I had a closet full for every season. But this hat was different, special.

Then, I lost my hair. Yes, just three months shy of my fiftieth birthday I was diagnosed with cancer. Not just any cancer, but an incurable cancer. Not just any form of an incurable cancer, but a very rare form. My children were eleven and sixteen. I was at the prime of my life. (How fair was this!) When I first lost my hair I put away my hats on the top-most shelf of my closet. Hats no longer felt comfortable. They would lie loosely on my bare skin and drop down to my hairless eyebrows. My head was always cold, though, so I would wrap it in scarves. I would sleep with crocheted skull caps on. I would not look in the mirror, at least not too closely. It was too depressing.

No sooner did my hair grow back and I would relapse. I was growing tired of hearing from my oncologist, "You have 3 to 6 months to live if you don't consider treatment." I had run out of family leave at my job. I had to go on disability. I had to have a stem cell transplant. I began to pray. Many others prayed for me and with me.

Then, my hair grew back and I reached again for that top shelf.

My family and I were going on the cruise of a lifetime to the Mediterranean. I could barely contain myself. It felt like an eternity since I had last traveled. My immune system was still weak and so was I. It was difficult to go out for fear of infection. It was only recently that I put away the surgical mask I wore in public. The prolonged confinement had been depressing. I was starved for sunlight and warmth all these months. I needed to feel like I could live again. There would be risks traveling, but I felt a cruise was a good option. There would be a doctor on board, and the food would be safe. I still would have to inject my medicine daily and keep it refrigerated, but our accommodations would provide for that. Once unpacked, I wouldn't have to repack for the whole trip.

How wonderful it was to be planning again, to have something to look forward to. So I went to the closet and turned on the light. I climbed the foot stool to reach the top hat box on the top shelf. With dust caught in my throat and my eyes moist from coughing, I pulled the box down and stepped to the floor. I had to brush cobwebs off the box. Then, I took a cloth, wiped it clean and opened it.

There it was, ten years old and no worse for the wear. I'd preserved its shape by having draped it over another hat. I lifted it out. It still felt silky. I looked into the hall mirror. My skin was sallow and my face thinner than before. My now salt and pepper hair was soft with short curls—chemo curls. I wondered if this hat would fit this funny head. I felt a tinge of sadness.

The person looking back was so different from the one I remembered when last she held this hat. That woman had been confident, happy. That woman could set goals and achieve them. That woman could get a "second look" from passersby when she wore that hat. With a sigh, I put it on my head and looked again, then closer. My eyes sparkled in a way I had not seen in a very long time. Was that a vamp or at least a strong contender? I could feel my spirits lift a weight off my shoulders. I was going to live again.

Just a few weeks before the cruise Dianne, my travel agent, called. She'd been able to upgrade us to two adjoining cabins with balconies and reduce our trip cost by $800. I knew this was going to be a very special trip! We would start off in Italy, visiting Naples first. From there to Malta followed by a day at sea. Then we would disembark in Barcelona and continue to Nice, France. Finally we would return to Italy to tour Florence and Pisa.

Hardly a day went by without some discussion of the upcoming trip among ourselves and with our friends. On the way to the airport, the cab driver couldn't help but stare at me and my two hats. Perhaps it was they that caused the ticket agent at British Airways to upgrade us to first class. We arrived in Rome blurry-eyed, my two hats still perched on my head and once on board the ship, I found a special place for them on a shelf by the dresser. I made sure my favorite hat was on top. The next day we were going to Naples, Italy.

The day was hot. The sun washed the color from the

ancient buildings. The four of us walked down the gangplank. At the end of the plank a photographer stopped us for a group picture. We gathered and smiled standing before a Naples banner. There was so much to see. Being a port, the city was right there. On the left was a fort-like structure. We climbed up the stairs and along the walls to enjoy a view of our ship and the town.

The street vendors in Naples were everywhere. It was impossible to pass up the gelato stands without trying some. The colors of lime, raspberry and peach were so enticing. The gelato was cool and delicious. The sounds of Italian, of motor scooters and happy people were everywhere.

Soon, we boarded a shuttle for a visit to Herculaneum. I held onto my hat as we walked a long, dark and slippery tunnel down into the ruins of the city. The air that rushed past smelled of must. It was such a contrast to that tunnel I remembered in Naples, Florida where our condo had been. This tunnel in Herculaneum led to an eerie stillness, a scene of great loss and devastation. Herculaneum was buried in mud from the famous eruption of Mount Vesuvius.

The slow excavation of the city revealed a community once very alive. We were surrounded by homes with brilliantly tiled floors and walls that displayed the wealth of this ancient center of trade. It was like traveling back in time. I could sense the anguish of those who perished so unexpectedly. I felt empathy and sadness. Without shade, the heat was relentless even with my hat on and we returned to the ship tired and thirsty. We found that there was a champagne reception in progress so we joined in. I put my hat on the back of a booth.

The next day I prepared for our excursion to Malta. I was dressed and ready to go; I just needed my hat. I shut the dresser door and turned to the shelf where I'd placed my hats. It didn't look right. I picked up the extra hat I had brought. There was nothing underneath it. But what was I thinking? My hat should be on top. I felt a tight gnawing rise from the pit of my stomach to my neck. I lifted the extra hat again. My hat was gone! My whole family searched both cabins. It was nowhere to be found, and we had to leave.

In my mind I retraced the steps of the day before. How could I have been so irresponsible? Back on board, I headed straight to the lounge. It was nearly deserted. I counted the booths to find the right one. Nothing. The lights were not on, so I began to feel around underneath the seats. I could feel the shallowness of my breath. I caught the attention of a passing staff member, and asked if he'd seen my hat. He said no, and suggested I go to the Bursar's office. There, I was advised to write a description of my hat and post it on my cabin door. The cabin staff would talk with others and it would certainly turn up. I made sure to point out the note to our staff. My head was throbbing. I couldn't stop reviewing the events of the day before. I couldn't stop thinking about my hat.

It was a day at sea. The weather was perfect. The ship had two pools and the four of us went to the pool deck, but I couldn't enjoy it. Everywhere I went, I looked for my hat. I had checked the Bursar's office in the morning and again after lunch, but no hat. In the afternoon a crowd gathered around the main pool to play group games for prizes. People were laughing. It was funny, but not for me.

I went to the upper deck to lie on a lounge chair and watch. The rest of my family stayed at the pool. It was a colorful group from my vantage point and I felt like I saw a hat on every woman, big floppy hats of lime and raspberry and tangerine. Then, when I was just about to put my head down, I saw mine. It had to be it. It was the only one like it, cool and sophisticated, not brashly colorful. The woman wearing it stood motionless.

I took my sunglasses off and wiped them clean. When I looked again, I could see the hat drifting away. There was no way for me to get up and reach it. She would be out of sight before I could get to the stairs. I couldn't be certain. Within minutes my family arrived breathless. "We saw it," my youngest daughter shouted. My husband had more information. "Did you see that woman? She was wearing your hat. I stopped her and asked her if she had found it and told her you had been looking for it. She said she didn't know about a lost hat. She said the hat was hers. Then she turned around and walked away."

Blood rushed to my head. I could feel my ears get hot. "Why couldn't you have stopped her?" I said. "Couldn't you have reasoned with her? I know that's my hat," I shouted. "For all these years I have never seen another one like it." But, of course, my husband was right and there was nothing that we could do. I didn't have my name in the hat and I didn't have a picture.

My heart broke. I had lost so much over the years, my joy, my health, my job and now my hat. And though it seemed silly, I felt like I would mourn it the most.

On the last night of our trip, I happened to walk through the gift shop area and on the wall were pictures taken during the cruise. I slowly scanned the many smiling faces of couples and families from every port of call. Then I noticed something I had forgotten, the picture of my family taken that day in Naples. There we were all smiling, and on my head was my hat. But it was too late now to prove the thief guilty. The trip was over.

All I could do was buy the picture. And when I got home, I framed it and placed it on my bookshelf.

— Roberta Frechette —
Frog Chant

They are nudging each other like bumper cars. It's the din of their croaking: tens, maybe hundreds of frogs that drew me from my walk up Winter Street to the entrance of the town forest. When I first approach from the gravel path I'm oafishly loud and they disappear in the leafy mud, but their business is life and death, so as soon as I remove my threatening shadow and settle down on the moss-covered tussock, they pop their bulgy eyes and sprawly legs up to the surface and resume their croaks and bumping. They're having a noisy orgy in the newly thawed marsh and it's a thrumming, snapping, boiling stew of shiny brown-green bodies. It's in the high sixties this late March afternoon and they have to party, now.

I try to recall if I've ever witnessed this spectacle and realize that I've never before had the time to walk and wander on a spring afternoon. These days I'm in treatment for cancer, six rounds of strong chemotherapy, and I'm too sick to work for the first time in my life. On good days, especially when my Robert is home, it feels like I'm on a well-earned sabbatical. I'll do yoga and strength training in my bright sunroom, enjoy the meals my kind friends have prepared, read inspiring books, write in my journal, and listen to music, guided imagery, or affirmations.

On bad days, often if I'm alone, or haven't slept well, I'll stay too long in bed, too fretful to do much of anything. Some days my stomach feels as though it's been scrubbed with a wire brush, and I have to distract myself from dwelling on my ravaged digestive system and "awfulizing" about a dark and painful future. I have every reason to be hopeful for a good long remission, but I still worry about the damage to my immune system from the toxic chemicals, and add layers of worry about the worry itself, until I don't believe its really working.

Today was a bad day. I was miserably wandering the quiet rooms, my focus reduced to my spine, imagining every twinge to be proof of the continuing presence of a dangerous lesion, even though my doctor told me that the last PET scan showed the cancer was responding and the bone was healing. I made myself get out of the house and walk.

There's movement at my left and I slowly turn my head and notice that new arrivals have hopped across the rocky path from who knows where, drawn by the outsized calls of the frog Town Criers. Some are already piggyback, and the bigger females, undaunted by their passengers, look for a safe haven for their eggs. I see one who didn't make it, its dry body flattened by a hiking boot or a mountain bike tire. Its once glistening round eggs are crisp, black, and two-dimensional, and the whole thing looks like an intricate paper cutout.

It's a dangerous business propelling a little soft body overland to get to the right pond on the right day. It would be overstated to say that it is frog courage that gets them here. It's more like a heedless devotion to life, a leap of faith, and I feel a certain kinship. Friends will tell me how they admire my courage, but I don't deserve the praise. I am afraid much of the time, and would weasel out of chemo if I only could. What the frogs and I know is that we are choosing life, and to do that means we sometimes have to cross a risky path.

The frogs lie on the surface of the water looking as smooth and naked as my bald head, and in my presence they seem comfortable. I'm the only sober guest at their party. It's not my kind of music and I don't get what the fuss is all about, but they know I'm watching and want to impress me with their seductive moves. "Pick me." Bump. "No, me." Bump—surely irresistible to one of the ladies of the lake and I feel honored.

The sun has gone down behind the pond and it's cooler. I've enjoyed the froggy frolics and am comforted. I'll leave them to it. By tomorrow they'll be gone, leaving only a few stragglers, back to their secret bogs far from the walking paths. For the rest of the season I'll be lucky to see one or two bob up or belly flop from the bank.

I stand up, a little stiff, and applaud silently, but the frogs have ducked under again. I decide to walk the long way home through the woods, gratefully, eyes and ears open. The mourning cloak butterfly, reborn today, lights on last fall's oak leaves; the tiny gypsy moth caterpillars writhe in their silken nests at the crotches of cherry trees. The blueberry buds are a rosy haze suspended above the marsh; the skunk cabbage unfolds its voluptuous purple and green speckled flower.

— Deborah Hemley —
Veteran

The doctor wore a white lab coat with two low pockets, stethoscope draped around her neck. Her pockets were bulging with pads, pens and a pager. She was attractive, with a young looking face, but based on the framed university degrees hanging on the wall, and a little bit of quick math, I concluded she wasn't as young as she looked. Her voice had an authoritarian, distant tone when she went down the checklist: "Any family history of heart disease, emphysema, diabetes, cancer, do you smoke, drink, how much, how often; what brings you here today?"

"I've been incredibly exhausted," I told her. "No energy. I go to sleep tired and wake up tired." I couldn't account for when it began or how long it had been going on. It had been gradual. For years, I had lived in a third floor walk-up apartment at the end of a long courtyard, a walk I did several times a day, every day with no problem. Now I had to stop on each landing and was winded when I reached the apartment. I was coming home after work and napping several hours.

"Are you depressed?" she asked. It was not the reply I had anticipated. "Being tired is depressing me," I answered. After some other perfunctory questions and nothing remarkable or noteworthy in my responses, she simply said the one-hundred-dollar diagnostic, non-comforting and non-reassuring words that "Everyone is tired; who isn't?"

I looked at her. She told me to come back if I started to feel ill, the message clearly that there was nothing she could do for me, no reason for concern here. Not from this tired woman doctor in the white professional coat, her waiting room crowded with sneezing, coughing, germ-ridden people in line for their turn to see the great doctor. I might not have known much, but this much I knew—I wouldn't be coming back.

I was very busy that summer, working a full-time job and planning my wedding. I spent weekends visiting florist shops, driving long winding roads to find a photographer's house, talking with the caterer about appetizers, roast chicken, braised fish, vegetables, salad, rice and a decadent chocolate cake. Under normal conditions this would be tiring. But this was more. I felt completely drained, no energy, and no reserve. I had to sit down wherever I could. I was dragging myself from place to place and sleeping at any opportunity.

A friend recommended a New Age type of clinician in Cambridge who specialized in vitamins and minerals. The receptionist gave me a board with a form clipped to it. I thumbed through the thick packet, skimming the text on the front and back of each page. Do you eat breakfast? Yes, cereal, juice and coffee. Do you smoke? No. Do you use drugs? No. Describe a typical lunch. Pretzels, yogurt and an apple. Do you eat meat or other protein? No meat—tofu, fish, cheese.

The vitamin man was nice enough. I'd seen many people who looked like him; trimmed short beard, polo shirt, chinos and Chinese slippers. As we talked, he was reading the answers on my form, repeating some out loud. "You don't smoke. Good." "Lunch, needs a little work," he muttered under his breath. I began to feel self-conscious when he started talking about mega-doses of vitamins and minerals. He prescribed 12,000 milligrams of vitamin C a day, which seemed excessive and humanly impossible to swallow. And he strongly recommended that I go on an elimination diet: no wheat, dairy, and no coffee, no anything I liked. "Do this for a month. I think you will see a big improvement in your energy," he said. "Then slowly add back, take these vitamins every day, we sell them here in our office—a convenience for our clients. We'll reassess the vitamins and doses on your next visit." A hundred fifty dollars later, I left with approximately 5000 tablets and a strict order to start the regimen immediately. I gagged three times a day trying to swallow the mega vitamins and was always hungry. Somewhere after a few weeks, I felt like I couldn't stomach one more vitamin, or one more bland meal, and eventually abandoned the whole thing.

Then, six weeks before my wedding, I was scheduled for a physical examination with my new HMO's primary care doctor. Although the timing wasn't the best, I was happy that I would be able to speak with someone else about my growing fatigue. I didn't know anything about this doctor's qualifications or areas of specialty; only that he was a male doctor, accepting new patients, affiliated with the local community hospital, and his office was three miles from where I lived. The exam was very thorough, and blood work was standard procedure. He told me that I would only hear from his office if there was something abnormal in the results, but didn't expect that would be the case. The following day while I was at work, I received a phone call from the doctor himself, telling me that my white blood count was higher than normal. "Come back in a week so we can redo the tests. I'd like to keep a watch on it. You're probably fighting a virus," he said.

I didn't give the conversation much thought. As I drove to the appointment the following week I was thinking about hors d'oeuvres, invited guests who hadn't RSVP'd and wondering if I had confirmed the musicians. The tests showed that the counts had gone up more. The doctor urged me to see a hematologist right away for further testing. I was too embarrassed to admit that I didn't know what a hematologist did.

My fiancé, Jon, drove me to the appointment for a bone marrow biopsy a few days later and for the first time, I told him how scared I was feeling. "What do you think they are looking for?" I asked. He said, "They're probably just trying to be thorough, I'm sure it's nothing to worry about." But I wasn't feeling so sure. The fatigue I had been experiencing didn't feel normal to me—it never had.

The hematologist, a serious looking young woman, introduced herself to us, and explained the procedure. I cried silently during the test, lying there on a cold table, in a sterile room, doped up on pain meds, admitting to myself that I had been worried for a long time.

I was alone when I phoned for the test results a few days later. The hematologist explained the findings of the biopsy. "Very unusual to see this type of leukemia in a young woman, most common in men over 65," she said, and proceeded to talk for a long time. I didn't remember hearing anything past the word leukemia. What about prognosis, expected life span, marriage, could I have a baby? "Are you okay?" she finally asked.

"This can't be happening," I said. "I'm getting married in a few weeks. Could the results be wrong?" "Let's schedule a time for you to come in, I think it would be better to discuss this in person," she said.

I lay down on my bed, and sobbed. I cried for a long time, feeling paralyzed and terrified. And when I didn't think there were any tears left, the crying started all over again. I finally stopped long enough to be able to pick up the phone and call Jon.

When Jon walked through the door, he looked heartbroken and scared. He took me in his arms to comfort me. "We're going to get through this together," he said. We held each other all night and only slept on and off.

"We don't know what causes it. It's a chronic leukemia with a life expectancy of seven years," she said. "Go have a nice wedding and honeymoon. When you return you can get more information and another opinion if you would like," she said. The implicit message was that the disease would be there when I got back.

The wedding felt insignificant. How could I go through with marriage when all I wanted was to grieve, locked away in my apartment? Family and friends stayed with me and talked me through the days. I had never felt anything like this before: desperately needing help from others, and left with little choice but to accept it.

The wedding was on one of the most beautiful days in September. I had always imagined my wedding would be a breath-taking experience, standing in a long white lace dress, enraptured by love, hope and possibilities. But this day was different. It was fragile. As I kissed and hugged guests, I saw us at a funeral, my funeral. As we made our wedding vows, there were eulogies playing in my head. At the sound of every camera snap, I imagined people looking at the photographs after I was gone. "Such a terrible, sad thing," they would say. "A pity. She was so young and had so much life ahead of her."

Now, thirteen years later, I've had chemotherapy, a bone marrow transplant, treated lists of side effects, experienced remission and recurrence, undergone new treatments and will undergo many more. I'm well versed in medical terminology and know how to ask hard questions and hear difficult answers. I'm not alone. I have my husband, daughter, family and friends; and a team of doctors who listen to me. I've feared dying the whole way. But, I've conquered it too, time and again.

While waiting for an IV in the infusion room at Dana Farber Cancer Institute, the nurse checks my name band. "That's an old hospital number," she says.

I tell her, "I'm a veteran."

Veteran

— Pat Connolly —
Simpler Now

I asked for this, so I have to sit down, be still, let it happen. I want to holler "No, some other day!" but I say nothing, so uncharacteristic of me.

The stool settles unevenly on the grass, tilting me a little left. I put my feet on the top rung, cupping my bare arches nervously around the wood. I scrunch my body, shoulders clenched, head bent down against my chest, both hands clutching the ends of the towel he's draped around my shoulders. What a slapdash version of a salon cape, I think. What a goofy send-up of the beauty parlor and its lustrous pseudo-glamour. Then he clicks on the clippers and steps behind me.

"Ready?" he asks gently. I feel tears sting my eyes. I nod and tuck my head a little lower on my chest. The vibration—solid, metallic, grim—moves closer, louder, til it touches me. The teeth of the clippers crawl up the back of my neck, inch into a mass of hair. No pain, I realize, no resistance. The hair is about to fall out anyway. Up the back of my head, cresting at the crown, the clippers growl along to the hairline at my forehead.

My husband stops, moves around me, beside me, then in front. I search his face for a cue. Unreadable. He breathes deeply, backs away a step, considers his handiwork. He doesn't smile. He makes no comment, which prompts neither comfort nor alarm. He moves behind me, the clippers humming in his hand. I feel the teeth against my neck again. Another row, and wads of hair dribble onto the towel, my legs, the grass. I stare, my heart jerking. So many shades, like those multi-colored guinea pigs—dark roots, natural red highlights, light brown dye job and blond ends bleached to straw by the summer sun. Harlequin hair.

Another row, and still he says nothing. I hold myself still, grip the towel tight, bite my lower lip. The cutting goes on, the clipper's groan fills the air. No early evening sounds. No dog barking. No music from a neighbor's house. Only this constant buzz surrounding us. Only us, him wordlessly harvesting this useless crop, and me, breathless, afraid to imagine what he's done.

He backs away again, his concentration melting into a smile, a big one. He cups my chin in his hand and raises my face. He looks from face to head, from head to face. Right now he could tell me lies, tell me nothing, tell me only what I want to hear. But the words he speaks right now are precious. They come from deep inside him, ringing with honesty. They feel like balm, like sweet, sweet honey. "I love it," he says. "Don't ever grow your hair again!"

I am simpler now. More bare. And I am loved. I still have two thirds of my left breast, I've hardly started chemo, no radiation yet. But I'm already a survivor. I cry and do not wipe the tears away. A breeze tickles my head in a place I've never felt it before.

— Cheryl Sisel —
All That Matters

I take out my suitcase, pack my clothing and breathing machine and drive to Long Island. My back hurts, my disk hurts, my legs are numb, my head is pounding but I keep on driving, and driving and driving, thinking of how they will run to me and yell "Bubbie, Bubbie, what did you bring me?" How I'll hug and kiss them, Zachy the tallest in his first grade class, so much like my son, Scott, and Avigayil, with her long curly hair, who reminds me of my daughter Amy, when she was five. Then, I'll bring them to the trunk of my car and give them their gifts and the Gushers, Spiderman Fruit by the Foot and the Dunkeroos that they love. We'll run in the house, sit on the living room floor, open the packages, the books I bought them, and play and play and read and read and all that matters is them.

On Sunday morning at 7 a.m. they wake me up by jumping on me in bed and yelling, "It's time to go to Central Perk."

I say, "Central Perk?"

"Yes!" they say in unison, "You know, the café."

I say, "It's too early," and they say "Get up!" and "Let's go."

Avigayil and Zachy swish through the green, red, yellow and rust colored leaves—all the leaves. I swish through them too and they say, "This is so much fun. Let's stay here and do this forever."

"OK," I say. "That's fine with me," and think then I wouldn't have to go the hospital for CT scans all the time, and feel sick and depressed. Yes, let's stay here forever and rustle through the leaves.

Suddenly, Zachy says, "I'm hungry. Let's eat." Avigayil says she is too. So we walk and giggle and tell silly stories the rest of the way to the cafe. It smells of the muffins on the counter. Zachy runs over and picks one from the pan. "Let me unwrap that for you," says the waiter. "I'll put it on a plate. "

I don't need a plate," says Zachy.

Avigayil takes a blueberry muffin, too, and sits at the table and we all eat the muffins. And then, after some French toast, we half-run, half-walk to the bakery.

I hold Zachy and Avigayil's hands, one on each side, and I think of how I want to live to see them grow up—become a Bar and Bat Mitzvah, get married, graduate college, have their own children. I don't want cancer to take that away from me.

But then, as we eat our cookies, I only think of how good the cookie tastes and that I'm with Zachy and Avigayil, and nothing else matters. I am breathing and eating a cookie and thinking about stopping for ice cream on the way back home.

Contributors

Harriet Berman is a psychologist who lives in Newton, Massachusetts. In 1998 she was diagnosed with stage one breast cancer, which was treated with surgery, chemotherapy and radiation. Formerly on the faculty of the Massachusetts School of Professional Psychology, she is currently the Program Director of The Wellness Community of Greater Boston. She credits her husband Stan and her children, Jessica, Jonah and Eliza, with giving her the spirit to survive and thrive.

Elaine Brilanstone was born in Roxbury, Massachusetts a few years ago. She attended Iowa Wesleyan College and Boston University and graduated from the University of Massachusetts, Boston, with a B.A. in Psychology and English. She received an MA from Lesley College's Independent Study Writing Program in Playwrighting. Elaine currently lives in Newton, Massachusetts, which to her, seems like "another world."

Pat Marley Connolly spent her first thirty years in Baltimore, Maryland, except during a four-year interlude in undergraduate school in Delaware. Before and after relocating to Massachusetts in 1984, Pat worked in various human service settings-mostly in work with adults with developmental disabilities. In 1999, she earned her Ph.D. in social work at Boston College, and later that year accepted a tenure-track position in Salem State College's social work department. She teaches social policy, research and other topics that students are least likely to enjoy. Pat lives in Reading, Massachusetts with her husband, Brian, two corgies, and on a part-time basis with two young adult children who both teeter on the brink of self-sufficiency.

Referred to as the "Martha Stewart for dogs," **Patricia Griecci** is the founder of Smiling Dog, a pet product design firm best known for its line of all natural dog treats. Smiling Dog received the Pet Pinnacle Award by retailers in 2001. Collaborating with Pets are Wonderful Support (PAWS), Pat created the "Pooch Party" chapter for Pads for Pets, published by Chronicle Books, the proceeds going to PAWS to help pet guardians living with disabling illnesses care for their animal companions. Patricia currently lives with her three rescue dogs, Spike, Sydney and Samantha-her smiling dogs.

Roberta Frechette, aka Brett, shares life, home, garden, and woods with Rob St. Germain, and, whenever they are around, her sons Jackson and Simon, and Rob's five children and two granddaughters. Roberta is the longtime Chef at the President's House at Wellesley College, worked as Food Consultant for the PBS children's program *ZOOM*, and combines her MS in nutrition, love of good food, and experience as a cancer survivor to create classes on Eating Well for corporations and community groups. She is also a member of the acoustic band, *Woodwork*, and the women's singing group, Constellations. Love, friends, good food, music, yoga, and writing, thanks to Peggy's class at the Wellness Community, help Roberta survive and thrive.

Deborah Hemley lives in the Boston area with her husband, Jon, daughter, Emma, and dog, Chili. She enjoys writing, yoga, reading and art. Her professional background and experiences are in social services, healthcare and website management. Deborah is a thirteen-year, grateful survivor of leukemia and an active participant at the Wellness Community in Newton. She credits the love and support of her family, advances in cancer treatment and research, along with a dedicated team of doctors to be able to claim the self appointed title of "veteran" in the battle against cancer.

Sazi Marden Andrew, Sophia, Cal, Ava and Chloe's grandmother, lives with her ever-traveling husband, Kevin, in Newton, Massachusetts. She grew up in the Independent Republic of Cambridge. She is a breast cancer survivor who works in the Lexington Public School as an Elementary Social Studies Specialist. She greatly enjoys the weekly yoga and writing classes she attends at the Wellness Community of Greater Boston. Sazi is especially grateful for having the great pleasure of working with Peggy Rambach in the Wellness Community Memoir Writing Workshop.

Originally from Pennsylvania, **Christine Micklitsch** has lived in Newton, Massachusetts for more than thirty years with her family. She holds a BS from Penn State, an MBA in Healthcare Administration from Boston University and is a Fellow in the American College of Medical Practice Executives. She has been the recipient of a number of awards and has published numerous articles and a book in her field. She receives her oncology care from Beth Israel Deaconess Medical Center, her Yoga from the Wellness Community and her faith support from Newton Highlands Congregational Church.

Cheryl Sisel worked over eleven years as coordinator of Keshet, in Newton's Solomon Schechter Day School library. Now, she volunteers there whenever she can. She is married to Joel Sisel, and is the mother of Amy and Scott, and grandmother of Zachy, Avigayil and Eitan.

About the Editor

Peggy Rambach is the author of *Fighting Gravity*, a novel based on her marriage to writer, Andre Dubus, and a collection of short stories entitled *When the Animals Leave*. She is the editor of *Seeds of Lotus; Cambodian and Vietnamese Voices in America*, also published by The Paper Journey Press. She was twice awarded the *Massachusetts Cultural Council Individual Artist Grant in Fiction*, was the recipient of the *St. Botolph Foundation Grant in Literature*, was a *Fellow at the MacDowell and Yaddo Artist Colonies* and named a *2005 Literacy Champion by the Massachusetts Literacy Foundation*. Ms. Rambach, is a resident teaching/artist in healthcare with grant support from the Kenneth B. Schwartz Center as part of the *Healing Arts; New Pathways to Health Initiative* in collaboration with the Massachusetts Cultural Council and the Vermont Arts Exchange. She lives in Andover, Massachusetts.

Breinigsville, PA USA
19 February 2010
232818BV00001B/4/A